W9-BUO-393

The Hip Guru's™ Guide to

The Stress-Free College Student

Natural Tips for a Happier Campus Life

Swami Sadashiva Tirtha, D.Sc.
Author of the Amazon
No. 1 Bestseller,
The Ayurveda Encyclopedia

The Hip Guru's™ Guide to

The Stress-Free College Student
Natural Tips for a Happier
Campus Life

By Swami Sadashiva Tirtha, D.Sc.
(Author of the Amazon #1 bestseller,
The Ayurveda Encyclopedia)

ISBN-13: 978-1495362521
ISBN-10: 1495362523

Cover Designed by: Madhav Karmacharya
Cover Photo: Girl meditating ©Copyright Hasloo
Group Production Studio
Cartoonist: Smaragdi Magkou
Publisher: Sat Yuga Press 132 Wilbur Hill Rd -
Unadilla, NY 13849 USA

The information in this book is for informational purposes
only. It is not intended to treat, diagnose, prescribe, or
cure any health condition. For all health issues you are
advised to consult a qualified health care professional.

Dedication

This book is dedicated to students in colleges and universities around the world who, for a variety of reasons, are experiencing the highest levels of stress on campus in recorded history.

I hope the insights in this book will help you realize you can return your stress to manageable levels, naturally, safely, and within minutes; enjoy a rewarding educational and social campus life that you will cherish forever; and build a foundation for graduating to the meaningful career of your dreams.

Image credit: <a
href='http://www.123rf.com/photo_25310992_crown-
chakra-isolated.html'>goku347 / 123RF Stock Photo</a>

Table of Contents

Foreword

Ask any college student, and he or she will tell you college is hard. But if college didn't make you do lots of thinking and learning, it wouldn't be worth it. And it's worth it. Take my word for it.

I was a college academic dean and professor for more than 25 years. During that time, I advised thousands of students. I also wrote a book that emphasized actions and attitudes that students require for success. Two of these are essential, but often overlooked:

Talk to advisers regularly.
Control your life. Don't let it control you.

Students rarely give time to either, claiming they feel pressured. What they don't realize is that not tending to these two points undermines academic success by *adding* to pressure.

Colleges are filled with advisers, including freshman advisers, academic advisers, others who help you choose a major, or still others who specialize in helping you research careers and jobs; however, students rarely seek them out. I've found that students who work with advisers succeed better than those who don't.

The book you're holding in your hands right now was written by an off-campus adviser you should really get to know. Swami Tirtha (The Hip Guru) is a stress-reduction expert. And he has written *The Stress-Free College Student* just for you.

If you follow Swami's wisdom and use his book as a resource, you can learn to control your life (see point number two above).

So many college students lead frantic lives. They're all over the place. They never seem to get anything done. They never seem to have enough time. They often don't get enough sleep. They scramble, rather than plan. They develop unhealthful, harmful, and self-defeating habits. They lose focus of their life and their goals.

The Stress Free College Student will become your personal guide to relieving stress, staying focused and alert, and caring for your mind and body.

Swami Tirtha has been a guru most of his life. He's a man of broad knowledge and deep wisdom—a generous and inspiring teacher. Through this book, you will certainly learn much from him about your life in general and your life as a college student in particular.

Without a doubt, when it comes to (1) experts who are worth listening to, and (2) developing a balanced life as a student, Swami Tirtha is *the* guide for you. He understands what you're going through and how to help you through it. He will show you how to put your college life in order and how to find balance and harmony in your *whole* life: mentally, physically, and intellectually.

Achieving this is more important than you think.

You might think of stress as being worried, nervous, and frightened. Although this is true, there is much more.

In the BIG PICTURE, stress is limiting. It inhibits
really being able to learn
really seeing your future after college clearly, and
really becoming an excellent person with rich and wonderful prospects at every turn of your life.

So use this book, take it to heart, and you'll find college to be a totally fantastic experience. This book is food for a vital life. Take my word for it.

~ *Dr. Bob*
Robert R. Neuman, PhD
"Dr. Bob" Neuman
Author of *Are You* Really *Ready for College? A College Dean's 12 Secrets of Success*

Image credit: <a
href='http://www.123rf.com/photo_23531945_lemon-soap--
oil-towel-salt-bamboo-and-candles-in-garden.html'>solerf /
123RF Stock Photo</a>

Acknowledgements

This book came about with the help of a truly awesome and caring team of coaches. I am most fortunate to have their support.

My coaches were headed up by Steve Harrison of Bradley Communications—an extraordinary person who helped me set my goals as high as possible and with the utmost integrity — and his crack team: Martha Bullen, writing coach who guided the craft of writing this material; Geoffrey Berwind, storytelling coach who reviewed each story to make them as engaging as possible for readers; Deb Englander, publishing coach who advised me on having the book presented in the most appealing and professional manner; Ann McIndoo and Mishael Patton who helped me structure my book and complete it in record time.

My college speaking coach, Tamra Nashman, helped me integrate my message with the book's message and urged me to get my book written now, not later.

Two coaches helped me develop my foundation vision and the message leading to this book: Raia King, my main coach who advised me on my message and presentation, and Mary Giuseffi, my branding coach, who helped tweak my choice of clothing that has students stopping me wherever I go to compliment 'my look'.

I'm also grateful to my friends and colleagues who took the time to edit the book for me, Robert and Jude Neuman, accomplished authors in their own right, and my editor, Guru Amrit Kaur Khalsa, who has been with me since my first book.

Any success of this book will be due in large part to my dear community of coaches, colleagues, and friends.

Introduction

It has been my experience that the most important insights – such as how I can most effectively help others – come to me serendipitously, out of the blue. This book was no exception. Having written two books already, one an Amazon #1 bestseller, *The Ayurveda Encyclopedia* that remained on their top 10 list for years, my current priority was to extend my keynote speaking to more colleges and universities.

My second book, *The Bhagavad Gita for Modern Times*, is a commentary on India's quintessential ancient book on Vedic wisdom. Many of my students had asked me to write a commentary to explain this renowned text using real-world examples so they could better grasp and apply its import.

Over the past 40 years, I have spoken at the White House Commission on Complementary and Alternative Medicine Policy, and at various colleges and medical schools, such as Johns Hopkins University, St. George's University School of Medicine, and Penn State University, where both students and professors felt a great affinity to integrative healthcare and consciousness. Those who approached me after my talks helped me see the interest and need for better solutions to health care. More recently, students and teachers began to share stories of just how stressed out the students were, bringing the need for natural stress-management to an all-time high.

It was this insight that motivated me to seriously consider speaking at more college campuses. As I began to prepare my presentation, I realized this material had all the makings of a useful guidebook for students; however, I was sure of one thing — students didn't need yet another book to read.

It came to my attention that the most popular and most rapidly growing activity for students was the website Pinterest — pictures and quotes that speak a million words. In that moment, the inspiration came to create a simple photo book with a few tips allowing students to glance through and quickly discover a useable tip. Add to that, stories from fellow students about how natural stress management helped them deal with college stress, and the book was formed.

May this book bring you inspiration and offer you solutions for a wonderful campus life.

Swamiji
Phoenix, Arizona
Jan. 26, 2014

Sincerity

Board 1
Student Workload:
Exams + Lifestyle

In a research survey I created and conducted of 100 college students attending SUNY Oneonta, the reported #1 college stress was workload and exams. This Board offers an inspiring quote and photo, natural solutions for relieving and preventing workload stress, and an inspiring story from one or more students who have relieved their workload stress by using wellness or stress-management tools.

Pin: Cartoon

Pin: Quote + Photo

Choose a job you love,
and you will never have
to work a day in your life
Confuscius

(Image labels: Family, Career, Life Balance, Health, Friends)

Image credit: <a
href="http://www.123rf.com/photo_15383198_diagram-of-
life-balance.html'> marigranula /123RF Stock Photo</a>
Quote added to photo

Pin: Natural Tips + Solutions

By keeping organized and prioritizing all areas of your life (not just studying) every day, you will be healthier, happier, and better able to deal with the peak stressors: Freshmen year, finals week, dating, senior career hunting, and pulling all-nighters.

Top 3 Foods That Increase Your Grade Point Average:

Garbanzo beans contain magnesium that has been shown to speed brain message transmissions while relaxing blood vessels. This legume even looks like a brain!

Broccoli contains choline (a plant compound) that boosts

cognitive function, learning, and memory.

Blueberries have antioxidants and other phytochemicals that improve learning, thinking, and memory.

Stop Studying For Better Grades + Less Stress!
EEG Neurofeedback
   Brainwave MP3's (15-30
   minute sessions)
      @ for improved memory
      @ for deeper relaxation
      @ for improved
concentration.

Good ADHD: Change it up—
      # each hour, stretch +
breathe

      # cross-study — like cross

training, change what you
study often

every 3 hours get some
fresh air for (10-30 minutes).
When you come back you will
get more work done with less
effort and find it all the more
enjoyable.

Hold on to what you love.
Talk to friends and
family.

Make time for hobbies.

Honor a well-rounded
life-study, play, socialize,
spend time in nature and with
the arts — in other words,
things that feed your soul.

Oh yes, now you have chilled,
go back to your studies and
you'll find you're much more
focused and ready to absorb
information.

Three Yoga Poses for Focus + Memory

Tree Pose
Pigeon Pose
Bow Pose

 See more tips on healthy foods, brain waves, ADHD, Love and Yoga at my website, Pinterest, Twitter + Facebook pages — see page 128

Pin: Story

You will read from your fellow college and university students, as well as a graduate student and a professor about how natural therapies helped them successfully deal with stress. I also shared my personal college stress story with you.

Swamiji's College Stress Story

When I was 18, something so stressful happened to me that it changed my life forever.

I was a counselor at summer camp in New Hampshire. One day the camp owner called me into his office and asked me to sit down. He paused, and then quietly said that he had some tragic news to tell me. He said my parents were in a car crash and they didn't make it. My parents had died. I was totally stunned. I told him I needed to be alone, walked out of the office in a daze and went for a very long walk down the forest road.

As I walked down the road, surrounded by tall pine trees, I

looked up to the sky and cried out to God, "Why, why!" but no answer came. And I kept walking.

I don't know how long I was out there. It was all a blur to me. The camp owner's son finally drove up and brought me back to camp. This must have been what they call the *dark night of the soul*.

I didn't think things could get any worse. Then the camp owner told me I had to tell my younger brother (who was one of the campers) about my parents, pack, help him pack, and then go to the airport to fly home. Having to tell my brother our parents were dead was the hardest thing I've ever had to do.

By the end of the day, our parents' closest friends, and our spiritual leader were there to comfort us. I remember sitting on a bed, holding the hand of a girl I was very close to.

Adults were in the room and we were deciding what to do, where my brother and I would live, and what to do about college. I had just completed my first college semester just before the summer. Some people suggested I stay home and get on with life, but I wanted my life to be as I knew it.

A few weeks later, I returned to camp, and in the spring I returned to my second semester of college.

When I returned to college after the mourning process, the workload became far more stressful.

I was majoring in TV and film, which I loved, but my heart had ceased to sing.

I found no joy in my studies, and although I had many loving relatives and friends, I felt empty without having my parents waiting in the wings.

While walking on campus one day — still in a fog — I fortuitously saw a sign for a lecture on meditation. Back in 1972, meditation was relatively new in America. We had learned that the Beatles went to India to learn meditation, but that was about all we knew.

So when the lecturer shared how meditation helps people find inner peace and mystical answers, I felt I had found what I was looking for.

It was a bit like a Star Trek TV show, and I was stoked to learn about improving my extrasensory perceptions and other metaphysical experiences.

I don't know what was better, the actual meditation or the information about higher states of consciousness that I would be developing. Whatever the reason, I felt so good. For the first time in my life, I felt a calling — a real purpose.

My experience was so profound that I wanted to learn all I could and share meditation with others. So for my fourth year of college I transferred to a different college, where I majored in teaching meditation.

For the past 40 years, I have studied and shared meditation, yoga, natural health, and related therapies.

And now that these concepts have gone mainstream, I am thrilled to share them with students now on campus.

Ironically, college stress is at an all-time high, just when natural stress-management therapies have become accepted and scientifically validated.

It is my great honor to help transform the college experience to a more manageable and enjoyable experience, so the next generation will have a better quality of life.

My greatest tragedy became my greatest gift. Although I would never wish such a tragedy on anyone, I'm grateful to share with you that from our darkest days can come beautiful things.

The Hip Guru's Guide to Seeing the Best in Every Situation — Including the Loss of Loved Ones

It is easy to tell someone in pain to not worry — to give intellectual advice. In fact, it is my observation that only when we experience pain in some way, can we empathize with others more deeply. Then when someone 'gets' your pain — your stress — when someone has gone through what we are going through, and has found a solution, we tend to want to listen to that person.

Many things were awakened in my life because of my parent's death. There is a phenomenon in the forest where when a pine tree catches on fire, the heat of the fire causes the seed in the pinecone to sprout and grow. I felt this is what happened to me. I had been set on fire, but I was now coming alive, sprouting a new life.

The intensity of the experience forced me to find a sense of peace and understanding beyond what the average freshman thinks about. And the intense pain and angst was the very thing that motivated me to seek solutions.

Now that I have cracked the code to virtually instant healing, the other important part of experiencing the death of my parents is to be available to help others who go through stressful situations and tell them its going to be OK; there are methods available to help relieve your stress.

In the 1970s stress-management options were

virtually nonexistent. Today, they are in every town and city. It is easier to find help these days than ever before.

 Links: More information on natural grief and loss management on my website, Pinterest, Twitter + Facebook pages — see page 128

Success in Any Undertaking

Image credit: <a href='http://www.123rf.com/photo_786933_success-a-hieroglyph-bears-success-in-any-undertakings-and-success-in-affairs.html'>mazurik / 123RF Stock Photo</a>

Board 2: Finances

Two matters share the spot for the second-most common causes of stress: finances + social life.

Both quantum physics and metaphysics say that everything is connected — inside of us and outside the entire creation. Therefore, it makes no sense to 'want' something, because you already have it — you are it and it is you. Quite a bit heady, but it is about tweaking your thinking patterns to say, I am full, clear out the old thoughts of scarcity (eg, I do not deserve money, love, happiness, good grades), and shift to thoughts of abundance: I deserve all forms of success, including health, wealth, love, and joy. Clear minds reflect more opportunities for success.

Pin: Cartoon

Pin: Photo + Quote

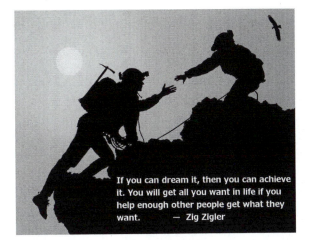

If you can dream it, then you can achieve it. You will get all you want in life if you help enough other people get what they want. — Zig Zigler

Image credit: <a href='http://www.123rf.com/photo_4116528_mountain-climbing.html'>pakmor / 123RF Stock Photo</a>
Quote added to photo

Pin: Natural Tips
Top 3 Mantras for Reducing Financial Fears

#Sham (rhymes with calm)
- calms emotions + nerves

#Aym (rhymes with (I'm)
- improves concentration and intelligence

#Som (rhymes with roam)
- gives vitality and joy

Top 3 Tools to Encourage Money to Flow Into Your Life (instead of rushing after it)

#Listen to hypnosis tapes that can retrain your limiting beliefs. You are worthy and have value.

#Keep a Feng Shui Money Tree in the rear left corner of your room (using your entry door as

the front) for attracting success

#Keep the rear left third area of your room/home/office/store neat and clean to allow financial energy to flow. If this corner of the room is boxed out (ie, a wall juts out), place a small mirror on the wall.

3 Foods for Attracting Abundance

#Lotus seeds

#Long noodles

#Bamboo

Links: More information on mantras, hypnosis, Feng Shui, abundance-attracting foods, see my website, Pinterest, Twitter + Facebook pages — see page 128

Pin: Story

One of the more stressful concerns of students is the financial burden they are amassing while in college. As seniors begin their job search, the stress can increase even more. A main theme in the stories you will read in this book is that natural solutions, from a rational or intellectual point of view, sound crazy! The following story is no different.

Feng Shui [feng is pronounced like "hen" with a 'g' on the end; shui rhymes with "Fay" and is pronounced like shway] is a popular science of organized structures (homes, offices, stores, etc.). Feng Shui is a Chinese concept that is used to design buildings and landscaping and keep them in harmony with nature.

Feng Shui, and its older science of structures, Vastu Shastra, from India, suggest that a building is a living, breathing entity, just like humans, animals, plants, and even rocks. Everything is energy and so everything is alive; however, there are various levels of energetic vibration.

Each area of the home relates to a different area of life — health, wealth, fame, career, helpful people, travel, love and marriage, family, creativity, children, and knowledge. If the energy flows, properly in these areas of the house, that area of your life will flow successfully. For example if you open the front door of your home and there is a foyer wall just a few feet from you, you will feel less expansive and relaxed than if you open the front door to a view of a great room with a magnificent view of a pond and mountain out the window.

Because these are universal ideas and because they make you feel better, many people will already be following some of these tips. And before you laugh off the idea that a messy, congested corner will block your wealth and prosperity, you may want to know that multibillion dollar corporations in Hong Kong, Singapore, and elsewhere in China, would never construct a building without hiring a Feng Shui expert. I figure if it's good enough for the über successful, it's good enough for me. I find it best to follow success templates rather than trying to reinvent the wheel.

One of the key benefits of natural, holistic, or integrative wellness is that it addresses the root cause of the situation. Many times, stress causes poor digestion making the body prone to many kinds of health conditions.

Sometimes, our thoughts tax our nervous system. Thus, the role of the mind must be addressed. Sometimes, it is the environment itself that is the core cause of stress. Imagine living next to a construction site with jackhammers and machinery making a racket all day and night.

The time-tested wisdom of ancient civilizations, such as India and China, tell us that all areas of our lives can be affected by our environment — from health, to career, to family and finances. The following story is how the structure of an apartment affected my client's ability to get a job and keep a job.

This may seem a stretch of the imagination. Yet, it works consistently. I am more interested in helping clients than attempting to not sound foolish. So I keep an open mind. If I am able to help people, safely, effectively, reliably and consistently with something, I use it. That is really what science is — repeatable actions, resulting in verifiable observations.

Albert Einstein said

"We cannot solve our problems with the same thinking we used to create them."

From countless case studies —
many from my own life, and
from the lives of my clients
over the decades, I share this
astonishing story of how the
layout or order of an
apartment can help or prevent
you from getting a job.

How a Healthy House Got Harry* Hired

"The reason you can't keep a job is because of your apartment!" That's what I told a client — his eyes wide open in disbelief.

"Maybe you didn't understand," he said, "I can't find work, and when I do, I'm let go within a month or so. I didn't come here to talk to you about my apartment — it's fine - no leaks or noises; safe neighborhood. I need advice on how to get and keep a job."

I told him I clearly understood his career issue and asked him to bear with me. I handed him a piece of paper and a pen.

I urged him to draw an outline of his apartment: "All will become clear in a few moments."

"According to Feng Shui, each part of one's home (office or any building) relates to some area of life. The space is divided into a 3 x 3 grid — just like a tic-tac-toe game. Based on where our main entrance is, the rear left third relates to wealth, the back third, relates to fame, and so on (see the map below)."

"One key to having all areas of your life healthy and balanced is to have each area of the building (home, office, etc), in harmony — meaning neat, clean, without obstructions, and most of all, no missing space."

"In your drawing your career section is missing, replaced by a stairway leading up to your apartment. You have no space for career in your apartment."

"Fortunately," I told him, "the Feng Shui solution is simply to put a mirror on the wall inside the apartment that is surrounding the stairs. This is symbolic of having the missing space restored and then the energy will flow properly in your career."

Later in the year I got a call from him.

"I'm so thrilled, just after placing the mirror on the staircase wall I got a job! And... I still have the job! It's the longest I've held a job since I moved to this apartment!"

* This is a true story of a session Swamiji had with one of his clients. Harry is a fictitious name for this real client.

Wealth Prosperity Self-Worth	Fame Social Life Reputation	Marriage Partnership Relationship
Health Family Community	Good Fortune	Children Creativity Entertainment
Wisdom Self-Knowledge	Career Life Mission Individuality	Travel Helpful People Spiritual Life

Front/Main Door Side of Building or Dorm

The Hip Guru's™ Guide to Feng Shui

So far, we have been reading stories about miraculous healings. This time, we stretch our belief system to include our home or dorm as a contributor to health, wealth, self-esteem, love, and spiritual growth. It is important to keep things in context. If you want good grades, you must study.

If you keep your wisdom corner harmonized, you give yourself an extra edge. In other words, ignoring the flow of your dorm room could prevent you from reaching your goals.

So if you want people to help you, help others. If you want love, give love. And if you want luck, be prepared when opportunity knocks. Cutting corners does not work in the long run, and it also keeps you from enjoying the journey, the adventure, and the building of one's integrity and character.

Here are a few ideas about how to apply Feng Shui to your dorm or college bedroom if you live off campus. Align the door to your room or dorm to the bottom of the chart. If the door is on the right side, it opens into the helpful people area; if the door is on the left, it opens in the wisdom area. If you are renting a home, you can map both your room and the home.

Basic harmonizing is not rocket science. While it is advisable to hire a consultant, you can get started yourself by searching online for tips. That's how I started. Then I brought in a specialist. Eventually I studied India's version of Feng Shui, Vastu Shastra, which overlaps with Feng Shui.

Best of all, the remedies are simple and inexpensive; so there is everything to gain and nothing to lose. What do you say! Enjoy Feng Shui!

Links: More information on Feng Shui + Vastu
Shastra — see my website, Pinterest, Twitter + Facebook
pages — see page 128

Wealth, Riches, Prosperity

Board 3: Socializing

Even when a student works out the social skills needed to survive high school, college is a wholly different culture. You are legally able to do things for the first time, such as drive and drink. Those who go away to school have the additional emotional challenges of leaving their social safety net. How do you discover yourself and grow wiser?

Pin: Cartoon

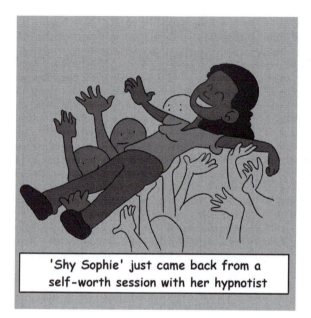

'Shy Sophie' just came back from a
self-worth session with her hypnotist

Pin: Photo + Quote

The wise make friends
with enlightened souls.

Vedic Saying

Image Credit: <a
href='http://www.123rf.com/photo_16425926_a-group-of-young-adolescent-students-boys-and-girls-around-a-table-with-a-digital-tablet-and-a-smart.html'>jesussanz / 123RF
Stock Photo</a>
Quote added to photo

Pin: Natural Tips
#Choose friends who

@ like you for who you
are. College is a time to
discover who you are.
You are your greatest gift
and your inner talents
can help you and the
world in unique ways.

@ are solution/action
oriented. If you want to
go nowhere, hang out with
people who complain and
find fault. If you want to
feel alive and purposeful,
choose as your friends
those who motivate you
and bring the best in you
out into the world.

@ encourage your dreams.
If we can dream it we
can create it. Dreams are
our inner voice reminding
us of our personal

abilities to be helpful and bring joy to others.

Disagreements — You can be happy or you can be right

@ Exercise your brain to see the best in people. Anyone can find fault and in the end, you will not have moved closer to your vision.

@ It is a sign of wisdom that you can consider another person's point of view and disagree, yet still respect the other person.

@ Life is short. Take every opportunity to find, live, and share joy.

Calm Social Anxiety

@ EEG brainwave MP3s help change the brainwaves from anxious in social and public speaking to relaxed in less than a 1-hour session.

@ NLP (Neuro-linguistic Programming) trains your brain to transfer good feelings to situations that used to make you uncomfortable.

@ Hypnosis helps you break old patterns that tell us we are not good enough, pretty enough, smart enough, or wealthy enough. And it helps us feel more self-confident about being ourselves around others. This can happen in just one session.

Pin: Reiki Story

One of the natural healing tools currently gaining popularity is energy healing. Massage and yoga, for example, relate to the physical body either through touch or stretching. The notion of energy healing, however, suggests a nonphysical connection between the healer and the client that results in healing.

Imagine the difference between a computer with a cable linking it to the Internet and a wireless connection. Invisible waves connect the laptop or tablet to the web. For that matter, the smart phone also uses invisible waves from cell towers to make phone calls and go online.

In the same way, energy healing is like a wireless connection. An energy healer can position his or her hands near a painful spot, (eg, a sore shoulder) *without touching* a person's shoulder for the healing energy to relieve the soreness.

Another useful analogy is the difference between air-blown heat and radiant heat from the sun, wood stove, radiant heated floor, or a space heater. Hot air blows and warms the air around the person, while radiant heat enters and warms the body but not the air. Energy healing enters the body much like radiant heat warms it.

Energy healing is becoming so popular and accepted that nurses at many hospitals use 'hands-off' energy healing on patients. There are countless ways to do energy healing. Each person can do it in his or her own way. There are also many schools that teach energy healing, where you can learn a systematized way to heal yourself, another person, or a pet. One of the most popular methods of energy healing is Reiki.

A Campus Reiki Story

Cristofre Martin, MD
Professor, Biochemistry, St.
George's University, Grenada

The day started off innocently enough, strolling across our beautiful campus with its pink adobe buildings and Spanish tiled roofs overlooking the aqua blue Caribbean waters and sky-blue sky. But as I entered my office building, the huge, heavy metal front doors suddenly changed my day. BAM! the door closed on my right foot, crushing it — especially my big toe.

I was with a colleague, and we both looked at my toes and each other in amazement. Right before our eyes we watched them swell up — like in a cartoon.

I limped around in pain for a while, then went home. I wanted this day to end, but as night arrived, so did more trouble. As I faltered around my home I noticed the toes blackened; I began to fear the worst: What if my foot was broken? What if my toenails fall off? Both the pain and the fears continued even as I went to bed for the night.

The next day, I had to interview someone for a position as chemistry professor, so I hobbled — in great pain and fear — down to campus and up to my office, paying very careful attention as to how I entered the building and passed through the doors. I made it to my office without further incident and collected myself as best as I could as I settled into my chair.

We began the interview talking about chemistry. After some time the interviewee handed me his CV, and I got up to photocopy it. The chemist couldn't help but notice me limping in excruciating pain, as I walked lamely toward the copy machine that was fairly close to my desk, although it seemed as though it were miles away. When he inquired about my condition, I told him how I had smashed my foot in the building's metal door the day before, and that now my toe was all blackened and very painful.

He casually asked me to put my foot up on the desk for a while. A strange request, but I humored him.

I had heard he was some kind of Reiki energy healer who gave a presentation on our campus at St. George's here in Grenada. I wasn't sure what Reiki was, but I was in such great pain and open to trying just about anything — especially if it didn't involve surgery.

When I rested my foot on the desk, he cupped his hands around my foot. And casually continued the interview as if everything was normal. We spoke about chemistry and what he could do at the university for us. He never alluded to the Reiki session he was conducting.

If anyone walked past my office at that moment, it would have looked very strange. But I was the chairman of the biology department, who would say anything?

Still, I'm a scientist and I'm a little skeptical about these things. But I went with it, and by 'it', I meant a 45-minute Reiki session à la job interview. I've conducted many job interviews, but this was certainly one for the books.

When we finally concluded our talk and healing session, I placed my foot on the floor. He left the office, and I went back to work. Aside from conducting the most peculiar interview of my life, I didn't give the event another thought as I began to take care of business matters.

Then, about 30 minutes later, something strange began to happen. I noticed that my foot became hot, as if it were wrapped in a heated blanket, or covered in Vick's Vapor Rub. My foot continued getting hotter — and I thought this was really strange, because there was no medical reason for this to occur.

So I sat there for another 20 minutes or so in my office while this was happening. When the heat finally subsided, I got up to go home, and lo and behold, I was walking without a limp! And there was no pain!

I couldn't wait to get home to tell my wife what happened. The foot remained better all day, right up until bedtime. I slept soundly, and the next morning I awoke to yet another *impossible* event. The toes on my feet were completely normal again!

They were pink and it looked as

though nothing had happened at all. When I got to work, I stopped by my colleague's office — the woman who was with me when I hurt my foot — and I showed her my foot. She was astonished. She said, "Holy mackerel, what happened? Your foot is brand new!"

I told her about the chemistry professor who zapped my toes with energy the day before. She then mentioned to me that she had a wrist problem that wasn't going away, and in the same breath, said that she needed to talk to this guy right away!

She asked for his phone number. She, too, was a biochemist and a skeptic, but interested. If Reiki could work miracles on my foot, perhaps it could help her wrist since nothing else was helping.

As for me, I had a healed foot and a more open mind to energy work. I had experienced a miraculous healing. At least, what happened was not possible by my understanding of medicine.

You don't go from a toe that is black and purple to one that is brand new overnight. At least you would go through a bruising period.

My colleague did get her Reiki session and experienced healing as well.

And my wife was so impressed with my healing that she became a Reiki healer, which really worked out well for me.

There have been times I needed other Reiki treatments. While we were traveling in Turkey, I threw my back out and was in such pain that I was bed-ridden. I couldn't get up, let alone get around the city. That night my wife did Reiki on my back.

Normally when my back went out, I would have been incapacitated for 4 to 5 days. But after the Reiki treatment, I was mobile the very next day, and I was well enough to walk around all day!

By the way, I hired the chemistry professor to work in my department (I'm no fool). Every morning we'd say hello, and I would get a zap of energy!

Who needs coffee any more!

The Hip Guru's™ Guide to Reiki

In the previous story the chairman of the biology department had the good fortune to have a Reiki master walk into his life and help his foot heal. Of course, this is a rare occurrence. Yet, if you start talking about Reiki among your friends, you might be pleasantly surprised to learn that someone very close to you practices Reiki or knows someone. When I gave a talk on natural healing at my local university, I ran into several teachers who told me they practiced Reiki.

Also, you can search online for 'Reiki Master' (your zip code or town, state) you should find a listing. Or stop by your local health store and you'll see business cards of energy healers, Reiki practitioners, and more that you can choose from. It's always good to ask for references from clients who had sessions with the practitioner.

Anyone can become a Reiki Master after just a few months of training. The title Reiki Master is a bit misleading. We usually think of a Master as one who has spent a long time mastering something, whereas each level of Reiki (there are 3 levels) can be learned in as little as 6 weeks.

Energy healing is used for most stressful or painful situations. We offer energy healing, de-stressing sessions for students at our local university just before finals week. Students walk out of their sessions floating on air, their stresses gone, and feeling better than ever. The next day, they come back for another session and bring a few of their friends as well. Others may have sprained ankles, burns, broken bones, or even serious illnesses, such as cancer.

People report their experience with energy practitioners, including Reiki healers, often takes away pain, swelling, and even illnesses. Nurses in hospitals use Reiki on patients who are nervous about their scheduled surgery to calm them down. Reiki is also useful post surgically to lessen pain or swelling.

The form of energy healing I do comes to me naturally. I call it *heart blessings*. Sometimes I invite a group of 20 to 30 people to sit together and help heal (or bless) one another. One woman reported that just 1 week after the heart blessing her doctor said her test results revealed she was free of hepatitis.

Another woman's doctor told her the tests showed she was had no more leukemia after 1 week. Of course I cannot guarantee this will happen every time to every person. The point is, our way of thinking about healing and illness is changing. As the research studies continue, adding legitimacy to alternative methods of healing, energy healing will become more accepted.

There are many doctors who have studied some form of natural healing, such as acupuncture, or who have had training in integrative medicine. They would be excellent professionals to see because they could provide more choices and explain your options.

For my last story, I chose an adult on campus rather than a student only because he comes from a Western (allopathic) medical viewpoint and has a healthy skepticism and a research background. One point of this story is that if someone with a scientific background believes something, it might give you the confidence to investigate whether energy healing will work for you.

 Links: More information on Reiki and other energy healing — see my website, Pinterest, Twitter, + Facebook pages — see page 128

Grace, kindness, favor

Board 4: Physical Health

When things get busy, we often forget the basic needs of life - things that keep us healthy. Here are a few simple, easy, and quick tips that can make you feel better instantly and prevent more stress and ill health.

Pin: Cartoon

Pin: Photo + Quote

"Healthy citizens are the greatest asset any country can have"
— Winston Churchill

Guided Visualization
Holistic Health
Reiki
Chiropractic
Energy Medicine
Yoga
Neurofeedback
Balance
Breathing
NLP
Hypnosis
Massage
Wellness
EEG Brainwaves
Integrative Medicine
Tai Chi
Acupuncture
Meditation
EFT - Tapping
Holistic Health

Image created by Swamiji

Pin: Natural Tips

Take a 45-Minute Vacation with Shiro Dhara (Oil Flow on Head)
   @ relaxes mind, nerves, and immune system

   @ makes you feel and look years younger

   @ puts you in a stress-free zone

Herbs for Health
   @ Ashwagandha for immunity

   @ Ginger/Licorice for colds

   @ Red clover for blood/liver cleanse

3 Secret Ways to Instant Health + Rejuvenation

@ Avoid white sugar and white flour products. All the natural nutrition has been bleached out of these products. (Whole cane sugar, honey, maple syrup, and whole grain breads are nutritious.)

@ Use muscle testing (kinesiology) to discover which foods are healthy for you and which weaken you.

@ Try EFT (Emotional Freedom Technique). It releases stress, pain, and fatigue in seconds!

Links: More information on Shiro Dhara, herbs, whole foods, kinesiology, and EFT — see my website, Pinterest, Twitter + Facebook pages — see page 128

Stories — Glories of Yoga

About 10 years ago, I owned a holistic health shop in a sleepy little village on the north shore of Long Island, NY. The space I was in was a cozy 300 square feet with huge picture windows. From my shop window, I looked out on the Long Island Sound and found it brought a great feeling of relaxation.

Among the items I sold in the shop was top-quality incense from India, which you could smell even without lighting the sticks. And instead of desks and chairs, I had white comfy couches so clients would feel more relaxed and at home.

Moreover, I arranged the furniture according to India's Feng Shui (Vastu Shastra) so the energy would flow and people would feel calm, energized, and alert.

Between the enchanting smells of the incense, the cozy couches, and the furniture laid out for optimal energy, people likened the experience to a mini-resort getaway.

For example, after an hour-long consultation, people would often remark before they left that they were already feeling better, even though they hadn't yet tried the herbs or other suggestions I made. It really makes your job easier when the environment does half the work for you.

At the time, I was holding small yoga classes for neighborhood residents. When I say small, I really mean small; the space only held 3 couples and me. The advantage of the intimate class size was that people got very personal attention.

One couple was very cute. The husband was very flexible when doing backward bends, but very stiff with backbends.

His wife, Amy* was just the opposite. She could do forward bending yoga poses, but could not do any backward bends. During their first yoga class with me — their first yoga class ever — Amy found it difficult to sit on her heels.

I had to give her 2 to 3 pillows to sit on so she could be comfortable. The next week — without doing any yoga at home — she was able to do without the pillows altogether and sat right back on her heels.

And like a child, Amy excitedly related stories how after the yoga, she slept so soundly for the next few nights that she almost overslept on Monday morning.

I assured her she was just releasing years of built-up stress and would not sleep through her time to go to work.

The next week Amy came back, again excited telling us that on the way home from work she found her car had a flat tire. Normally she would have gotten so angry and tense and stayed in that mood for days. Yet somehow, seeing the flat tire that evening, she didn't get bent out of shape. In fact, she just calmly thought what she needed to do to get her tire fixed and get home to her family. She was thrilled, sharing with us how the yoga helped her become so calm and relaxed.

It was very rewarding for me to see how one simple yoga class a week could so transform the quality of peoples' lives.

Now, 25 year later, Amy shares her update. She is now in sales:

"I am able to draw on my experiences with yoga and meditation and allow myself to focus on the fun side of meeting new people, using my brain, acquiring new skill sets, and simply enjoying the ride.

Yoga has been an invaluable asset for me in all aspects of life. In this business, it helps me to keep things calm and helps me focus on solutions.

Most people are not surprised when they find out that I am into yoga and meditation. I enjoy sharing it with friends and colleagues, especially if it can help them with a health issue or stress.

My own practice is not what it was, but I still practice daily, but on a more limited basis. It is something I see as a gift that I can share. You inspired me with the spiritual aspect, and I cannot imagine doing yoga without that."

Back to my yoga stories:
The form of yoga I teach is gentle Hatha Yoga. I encourage clients to move only into the poses to the degree that they feel comfortable.

I remind them that yoga is not a competition with your neighbor; it is not a race; and the "awards" won are enhanced mind-body ease, flexibility, health, and joy.

Once while traveling I gave a yoga class. A father and his son attended the session. The class proceeded as normal. People were feeling comfortable enough to just stretch to the extent their bodies allowed.

After about 30 minutes, the son, Eddie* spoke up. He said, "This is the first time I have tried yoga and I have to tell you something. I am a recovering heroine addict, and I feel better from this yoga than I ever did using heroin."

I'm not sure which stunned me more, that a high school boy was

recovering heroine addict, or
that yoga made Eddie feel better
than this addictive, crippling
drug. Either way, I was so
grateful that he found a safe
and natural way to feel good
about himself.

Yoga, meditation, life purpose,
taking action to fulfill life
purpose, laughing, and thinking
positively are but a few of the
scientifically proven methods by
which the brain can produce
natural calming chemicals in our
bodies — dopamine, serotonin,
endorphins, and oxytocins. These
chemicals make you happy by
eliminating depression and
quelling pain.

Takeaway: Do daily actions that
increase these natural brain
chemicals so you feel happier
each day. Surveys have found
that 50% of college students

have some form of depression. Get in front of the curve and dissolve depression now — or prevent depression by tweaking your lifestyle by adding some happy acts now.

*Amy and Eddie are fictitious names of real people who shared these stories.

The Hip Guru's Guide: Yoga Benefits

In these two stories, we see how in even a short amount of time doing yoga has profound benefits, both immediate and even decades later to help relieve stress well into your first, second, or even third career.

 See pg. 128: tips on yoga at my website, Pinterest, Twitter + Facebook. Also, my #1 Amazon bestselling Ayurveda Encyclopedia, has an entire chapter on yoga poses.

Health

Board 5:
Emotional Health

Feelings may be our best way of knowing our truth. If we feel something, we know it. A sunset makes us feel peaceful; a baby makes us feel joyful. Tuning into our feelings are a great way to know if we are OK or need some love and joy.

Pin: Cartoon

Pin: Photo + Quote

If you think
you can do a thing
or you think
you can't do a thing...

You are right.

Henry Ford

Image credit: <a
href='http://www.123rf.com/photo_9727016_view-of-smiling-
man-raising-his-hands-while-standing-in-the-
field.html'>pressmaster / 123RF Stock Photo</a>
Quote added to photo

Pin: Natural Tips

Do Nothing + Feel Better!
   @ EEG MP3 sessions
   calms emotions and stress
   in less than 1 hour.

   @ Guided Visualizations -
   sit in a quiet place and
   imagine yourself in the
   most peaceful, loving
   place in the world!

   @ Meditation — repeat a
   word, mantra, or image
   you love to bring yourself
   more love and peace.

Indulge Your Senses + Feel
Better!
   @ Color therapy — Blues
   end the 'blues.' Sky blue
   calms and re-connects
   the emotions. Add blues
   to your life in the form
   of wall paint, pictures,
   sheets, and clothing.

@ Aromatherapy — Use sandalwood oil for calm + memory. Put it under your nose, on your pillow, or on a light bulb.

@ Gotu Kola herbal tea, a calming brain herb. Drink it 2 to 3 times a day.

Foods that increase your GPA

@ Milk/yogurt boost memory neurotransmitters

@ Blueberries have antioxidants that boost memory

@ Walnuts — omega-3 fatty acids - facilitate learning + memory.

See more tips on my website, Pinterest, Twitter + Facebook. Also, my #1 Amazon bestselling Ayurveda Encyclopedia, has an entire chapters on these subjects — see page 128

Pin: Story

This story is a little different from the previous ones in that, despite the stress-management techniques she used, this student is still experiencing gripping college stress daily, even as she prepares to graduate.

However, this is an important story because there are many students in the same boat. Despite their following natural stress-management methods, challenging issues persist.

The good news is that there are solutions. There are ways to reduce stress to manageable levels. It requires taking the time to search out more effective solutions that work for you. More about this after you read this story.

Stressed-out Student Composer Hears the Music

Li Li* the Graduate Student

I think stress may well be my middle name. There are so many layers of stress that it may also be my first and last name. First, this is only my fourth year in America; I was born and lived my life in China. So I have additional stresses adjusting to this culture, and further, I have to learn technical vocabulary in my courses. It's like having to learn two new languages.

I came to the United States and relocated to New York City to go to grad school. The adjustment to life in NYC was another huge stress. My college major had been graphic design.

But I have been composing and recording my own music since high school. I thought it would be exciting to get a Masters degree in music and become a composer for the film industry. And so it seemed like an exciting idea to enroll in a graduate school for music.

The first day of classes, my excitement instantly turned into terror. The teachers informed us we have to learn the fundamentals of music — the physics and math of how sound waves travel and how sounds produce effects and how to program music on the computer. 75% of the program was physics and math; 25% was music. But I'm an artist!

I have no experience in the sciences. I could feel the stress pour into my body — my bones, nerves, and brain. I was totally unprepared for these additional layers of alien studies. In fact, except for a few of my classmates who came from engineering or programming background, the whole class was stressed out. I was sitting in a room of music students who generated stress. The atmosphere was toxic! We thought we had signed up for arts and instead got mostly science.

That first semester was really tough; the stress was intense. I cried a lot. Fortunately, my classmates helped me out, especially those who were in their second semester. They said it gets easier after the first term.

They were right: the second semester was much easier. But

campus life was still highly stressful; and I still had my cultural and language issues to deal with.

What I found to help me, what I use to this day, is a combination of stress-reducing techniques. During my first year, I lived near Central Park, so I would take long walks in the park. This helped me clear my mind. I also took hot baths every day while listening to brain-wave tapes, called "binaural beats." That also helped me quite a lot.

If I felt really lost and not sure what to do with the enormous, paralyzing workload — so many projects to work on — I would write about what was stressing me out.

This helped me to prioritize what

needed to be done and to cope with situations that I didn't know how to handle.

I share a house with some classmates. I wish I could say that the stress management solved my issues, but it just took the edge off — then a whole new level of stress grabbed hold of me.

I'm supposed to graduate in the spring. I have a challenging thesis to complete. And then I have to think about getting a job.

Composing for the film industry is one of the most difficult fields to get into. You could starve for years before you can even get a break. That's really not for me.

So I decided to major in music computer programming. I might be able to integrate this training with my graphic arts training and do some things for websites.

It is a more stable life, and I really need that now.

The stresses are so great, my mind and body are tense all the time. My hands are always shaking; my heart is always pounding. Just thinking about my thesis and finding a job keeps me in this state all day long. Then the normal, daily stresses of city life and personal relationships just make things worse. I've tried so many therapies. So far, baths, walking, and binaural beats have helped me most.

* Li Li is a fictitious name used for the real person who shared her story with Swamiji.

A Happy Ending
When Stress Management Offers Only Partial Help

When Li Li finished relating her experiences, it was clear that she was still suffering from intense stress on a daily basis. The other stories all have happy endings. I wanted Li Li's story to have a happy ending, too.

After listening to her story. I offered her an EFT (Emotional Freedom Technique — see page 63) therapy session right then and there on Skype. She accepted, and in less than 30 seconds — even before we finished the minute-long session — she said she was already feeling better.

After the 60-second session was done, Li Li said she felt her stress level drop from 7 out of 10 to a 2 or 3 — a manageable level...a happy ending.

What makes this story so important to relate is that Li Li and many other students, even after using relaxing tools, are still experiencing overly heightened stress levels day after day. I feel it's important to speak about how to find a solution to reducing ongoing and high levels of stress.

The point to highlight here is that there <u>are</u> effective solutions — it just takes time to find what works best for you.

If this is your story, too, I suggest you share it with your parents, teachers, and counselors to give them a better feel for what you are actually going through. Emotional support, as we learned from Li Li, is quite valuable.

Also, if you don't have the time to seek out more effective therapies, perhaps your family can help, or your teachers or counselors may know someone who can help. When I visit college campuses, I meet many college professors who are trained in various natural stress-management therapies. Help is closer than you may think.

If you have a local health food store near your college, look on the bulletin board and you are likely to find many listings for practitioner. Also Google "natural stress management + your zip code" to see who offers solutions near you.

The Hip Guru's Guide to Brain Entrainment

One of the most helpful therapies for Li Li was listening to "binaural beats." These are one of a series of sound therapy options that fall under the heading of Brain Entrainment.

There are sound machines that play binaural, monaural, isochronic, and alpha, beta, gamma, delta, and theta waves that literally alter the brainwaves. Just as combing your hair makes it look more orderly, so too, listening to these sounds "comb" the brain waves into more peaceful, calm, focused waves. Different wavelengths have been researched and found to help various conditions, from physical pains and illnesses to mental or emotional issues, such as ADHD, inability to focus, and anxiety.

Different wave patterns help you think outside the box, enhance creativity, alleviate pre- and postgame stress, relieve social anxiety when meeting new people or before public speaking, and help you overcome sleeplessness, to name a few.

There are many scientific studies on the benefits of these cutting-edge brain entrainment sounds. A more recent technique is the use of light-therapy glasses, which permit lights to flash in sync with the sounds. This gives a dual-sensory experience and further deepens relaxation and entrainment.

There are a few precautions. First, entrainment is not to be used with people who have a history of seizures (such as epilepsy). Also, the sounds should not be listened to while driving or operating heavy machinery. In short, it is best to listen while you are sitting relaxed in your home or lying down.

 See more tips on brain entrainment at my website, Pinterest, Twitter + Facebook — see page 128. Also, my #1 Amazon bestselling Ayurveda Encyclopedia, has an entire chapter on yoga poses

Joy

Image credit: <a href='http://www.123rf.com/photo_7678492_chinese-calligraphy-character-joy.html'>seiksoon / 123RF Stock Photo</a>

Board 6: Spirituality/Self-Worth

However you define spirituality, spend more time with it. For some, it means religion. Spend more time with your religion. Others feel spirituality is a more universal idea of giving love, care, and joy; loving yourself, others, and the planet.

Pin: Cartoon

Pin: Photo + Quote

Be Yourself

Everyone else is already taken.

Oscar Wilde

Image credit: <a
href='http://www.123rf.com/photo_13766021_young-lady-
expressing-her-desire-for-freedom.html'>sangoiri / 123RF
Stock Photo</a> Quote added to photo

Pin: Natural Tips

It's Healthy to Run Away!

@ Who am I? — Take some quiet time to find out what makes you tick, and get in touch with that unchanging person inside you who has been there while your outer self has grown and changed.

@ Nature - Spend time around trees, mountains, rivers, oceans, planets + stars, and wildlife to re-connect and find peace and wholeness.

@ Pets + Plants — Caring for something helps the heart grow louder and thoughts grow quieter.

Lighten Up — Attitude Adjustment

@ Tell jokes, make up jokes. Laughing releases

brain chemicals that release stress, increase health, and promote a healthy outlook.

@ Attitude of gratitude — See the best in every situation — (If you really can't — laugh about it).

@ Get out of your own way. It's easy to blame others. It's wiser to see how things improve when we change ourselves and our habits.

3 Tips for Improved Self-Worth

@ Watch your thoughts without judgment. Sit quietly and see where your thoughts lead you

@ Serve. Help others in need. Give a hand up; teach, build, play, share

@ Act. Put your dreams and visions into action. Create your reality in the world.

See more tips on my website, Pinterest, Twitter + Facebook — see page 128.

Pin: Story — Purpose, Dreams + Time Management

This is an important story for freshmen who are new to the campus culture, experiencing being on their own for the first time in their life, and away from social support networks and home.

Following the simple 3-step college preparatory plan of the Hip Guru's™ Guide will save

you unbearable stress,
isolation, confusion, and going
down the path to failing
grades.

1. Clear out the stress and
   confusion using any number
   of stress-management tools
   discussed in this book or
   elsewhere. When the
   emergency is finally under
   control, you will be able to
   think clearly.
2. Find your Life's Purpose.
   Find out what brings you joy
   and what you would pay to
   do because you love it so
   much: Major in that! Back on
   Board 1, I posted a relevant
   quote from Confucius: If
   you do what you love, you
   will never work a day in
   your life. This applies to
   college, too. Doing what you
   love is fun. Being happy also
   makes you productive.
   Corporate wellness research

has proved this. Doing what you love adds value to the product or service you develop. People are willing to pay more for quality products. Now that you have your target, what actions (and in what order) will you achieve your goals?

3. Goal Planning + Time Management: Create short-, mid-, and long-range goals and journal your to-do list daily, checking off the steps completed.

Review your to-do list and prioritize it. This template permits smooth running of your life for the short and long term.

You can always amend the plan as you see fit. It is better to have a plan and change it than to have no plan at all.

1. For school, list and prioritize the homework you have based on the deadlines and difficulty of the work.

2. What other work or research is required to complete your assignments?

3. Schedule time for eating healthy meals. You need only take 10 to 20 minutes to cook and complete a healthful meal.

4. Schedule time for exercise — even 10 to 20 minutes every 1 to 2 hours.

5. Ensure you have some social time, time in nature. And call home.

Freshman Frances
Music to Her Ears

Freshman life was a real shock for me. I was away from home, free to do what I wanted, with no parents telling me what to do; I had enrolled at university with a vision to become a music composer and producer. But with all this freedom, out went the dreams and in came the parties, alcohol, and weed.

Homework assignment deadlines loomed, but every time I thought about the deadlines, the tenser I became. I felt overwhelmed.

I needed to make a decision about what to do, and found I kept turning to the same solution: procrastinate.

My habit was, if I weren't in class, I would hang out with a party crowd at school, at the beach, or at someone's home.

When I was alone in my own off-campus apartment that I shared with other students, I would spend my time sitting on the bed surfing the Internet, or lounging on the couch in the living room playing video games and zoning out. Zoning helped ease the tension, at least in the short term.

Eventually I remembered my homework deadlines and the stress rushed back into my life — and into my chest. I would be tense and anxious for a while. But then I would return to my "MO": procrastination. If I could just sweep the problem under the rug, I would forget about it.

This strategy seemed to work for the first month of college. Then reality knocked on my door. Actually, it arrived by way of my college grades. I was failing classes!

Fortunately for me, an angel stepped in. My father sent me an email pep talk just when I needed it most.

I was motivated! I began exercising again — this helped me cope with the stress.

I was able to break out of the procrastination mode by doing my work ahead of time. I also stopped smoking weed, hanging out with the party crowd, and got on top of my workload.

Remembering my dreams,
I began focusing on my music.
Playing more music also relieved
my stress; so did switching from
video games to playing with
music production software.

I began to align myself with my
highest standards of living. I got
out of the house more, and made
new friends with other students
who live by their highest
standards.

It's month three of my freshman
year, and these tools have been
a big help for me. I could still
use some more stress-relieving
tips — especially how to deal
with anxiety attacks when they
arise. Overall, I'm proud of
myself for turning my life around
so quickly.

*Frances is a fictitious name of the person who told this
story.

The Hip Guru's Guide to Living Your Life Purpose and Dreams

Frances is a remarkable person to have been able to turn her life around in just 3 months. The statistics bear this out. Nearly 50% of college students feel some form of depression, and many students turn to drugs and alcohol to deal with their stress levels. And 50% of student fatal car accidents result from alcohol. Hopefully, these statistics are a wakeup call for all students.

Frances' turnaround story offers an inspiring story showing that it's possible to get back on track after making some ill-advised choices. Her story also illustrates how she did it. There are no big mysteries. It involves having loving family and friends in your life, connecting to your life purpose, and taking constructive action to attain your dreams.

After I interviewed Frances, I asked her if she had any questions about stress management since she was still looking for better ideas.

She asked me how to deal with the anxiety attacks. I suggested "the tapping or EFT technique" that I shared in the last board. In 60 seconds or less, you can feel the stress drop to manageable levels. Here is the link to watch the video: http://thehipgurusguide.com/melt-stress-in-60-seconds-or-less/

Because she knew her joy was in music, I helped her sculpt a vision for short-, medium-, and long-term goals that would delight her and that were within reach.

Then I suggested she journal each day to help toward reaching her three primary goals, and record what she needed to do the next day to move toward living moving closer to her goals.

Other tips included eating healthy foods, doing yoga or tai chi, meditating, and keeping a bottle of "Rescue Remedy" nearby for instant relief (see website for links).

Socially, I advised her to join meet-up groups for musicians, entrepreneur musicians, and small business owners; and to take electives in entrepreneurism, business, and the web business.

Finally I advised her to read more books on self-worth to attract abundance and to read biographies of famous people to learn how they faced and overcame challenges and seized opportunities as they moved toward achieving their dreams.

Remember, it is easy to do if you clearly define what brings meaning to your life and then take daily actions — however small — to realize your dreams. Support groups and a healthy lifestyle round out the success template for your best life. Living life with purpose raises your self-worth.

 See more tips on these topics on my website, Pinterest, Twitter + Facebook — see page 128.

Peace

110

Board 7: Summary
Understanding — Action —
Integration

I've shared these quick tips to
help you de-stress, survive +
thrive in 6 key areas of life. If
you have tried even 1 of these
tips, you likely have found it
beneficial. If you are reading
this, you probably have found
some miraculous stress relief
to have encouraged you to
continue reading to this point.

Taking action is the key to
accomplishing anything. We
can read and think, but action
and experience are necessary
to see the results of our
actions, only then can we
know if something is true for
us, or if it were a theory
proven wrong. Here you'll
integrate the tips holistically
into your life.

Pin: Cartoon

Pin: Photo + Quote

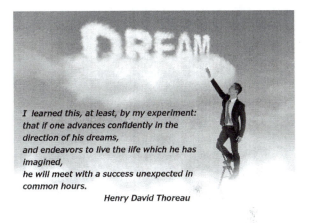

I learned this, at least, by my experiment: that if one advances confidently in the direction of his dreams, and endeavors to live the life which he has imagined, he will meet with a success unexpected in common hours.

Henry David Thoreau

Image credit: <a href='http://www.123rf.com/photo_12652584_businessman-climbs-ladder-and-get-his-dream.html'>ximagination / 123RF Stock Photo</a>
Quote added to photo

Pin: Natural Tips

Workload is eased when we have

    @ less stress

    @ more sleep

    @ more self-worth/confidence

    @ eat healthy foods

    @ have a pleasant social life.

Finances are better when we

    @ do not fret over money

    @ manage school and a job

    @ save and spend wisely

    @ buy fresh foods in bulk rather than pre-packaged foods

    @ have emotional stability so we don't eat and buy to gain self-worth

    @ gain spiritual stability so we don't eat and buy when we feel spiritually empty.

Social Life is better when we
    @ take time from our workload
    @ are physically healthy
    @ are emotionally calm
    @ do not overspend
    @ have spiritual grounding and self-confidence.

Physical + Emotional Health is better when we
    @ eat healthier foods at regular times
    @ are not stressed or worried
    @ have a balanced workload and social life
    @ feel spiritually connected and self-confident.

Spiritual life is better when
    @ we make self-confident decisions for our work, finances, socialization, and mind/body health.

In short, everything influences everything else. Nourish each area of your life and you will have a wonderful, well-rounded life.

See more tips on my website, Pinterest, Twitter + Facebook — see page 128.

Pin: Story
The following is a story of a recent graduate who used breathing, life-management skills, and re-programming tools to deal with his stress, and lived to tell about it. He tried several methods, from merely thinking himself into success (which didn't work) to connecting with nature and color therapy (which helped him quite a bit more, but still not enough).

Continuing to search for a solution, he finally found some MP3s online. He downloaded them and learned even more effective life-management skills and breathing techniques.

Now you may ask, "Why does someone need to learn to breathe; isn't breathing automatic?" The answer is, yes. It is built-in, automatic; however, when we get stressed, we shut it off. We stop the natural breathing process. As simple as it may sound, breathing is perhaps the most important and effective relaxation tool you can use.

An Animated College Stress Story

I recently graduated from an online animation school I had attended for the past two years. Homework assignments involved creating animation shorts and submitting them. These weekly deadlines caused me a lot of stress.

My challenge was how to hit the required goals, while not freaking out. In the early days, one tool helped a bit: As I worked on my latest assignments at my bedroom desk, I could look up at a poster on the wall of a rainbow descending onto an island in the middle of the water.

Above the picture, in big letters was the word *EFFORT*.

Below the rainbow were the words,

"Go the extra mile." My college teacher had given me this poster, and it helped inspire me as I worked on assignments. "Go the extra mile." Easy for my teacher; not so easy for me with my stress levels!

So, I realized it was time to try some new stress management skills: first, I switched to doing my homework during the day, because my mind could focus better and my eyes were fresher. Second, when I got confused or anxious, I would look out the window to my left, and stare at the sky. The sky-blue color calmed me down and made me feel connected to everyone and everything.

These strategies — basic stress management tools helped to a degree, but when the assignments got me really stuck, my stress levels would get almost out of control.

I remember one particular assignment where I had to animate laughter. It was very challenging. I had not animated laughter before the assignment. I kept trying but the animation didn't feel right.

This is what happened with my other projects. Each time, after a few failed attempts to create a part of the animation, I got stuck and began to feel frustrated and blocked. Over time, I found myself getting increasingly short tempered, not only with other people but also with myself.

I would say things like, "What's the matter with me; it's so simple, why can't I do this? Why am I spending so much time on this? Will I be able to complete this before the deadline? What if I don't finish before the due date?"

These questions constricted and tightened my chest.

I would then feel even more stuck. This frustrated, blocked behavior pattern might last for hours and hours as I berated myself and wallowed in panic, still totally unproductive.

Then I came across several online podcasts about how to relax and not get stressed. I began to try some of the relaxation methods mentioned in the podcasts. The first method said to move away from a situation that is causing you stress.

Walk away and do nothing; lie down and breathe. I didn't know how this would help me solve my animation dilemma.

But I had to do something. I tried

it. At first it felt funny; how is walking away from the stress going to help me finish the homework? It didn't make sense. But I was so tense, I knew I needed to try something different.

And so, I tried it—lying on my bed and breathing. At first the exercise made me realize I was not even breathing—I was in such a panic. And then, slowly, it began to work! After only 10 to 15 minutes of deep breathing, I calmed down.

Then I would return to my work and try to figure out the problem again. If it still didn't work, I at least maintained my calm and presence of mind.

I then decided to move on to some smaller, easier parts of the assignment to rebuild my confidence.

After some time, while not focusing on the problem, working on other topics, the answer to the problem would often come.

Other times, when I completed the other parts of the homework and I still had no solution, I realized I could go online ask my fellow classmates or my mentor for help.

And so, I taught myself how to handle situations where I felt blocked. Occasionally, I was unable to finish the work on time. And you know what: the world didn't come to an end.

Yong Kang, the "Nerdy Creator," is the author of the upcoming book *Fearless Passion: Find the Courage to do What You Love*. http://www.nerdycreator.com

The Hip Guru's™ Guide to Thought Training + Time Management

There are some great lessons we learn from Yong's experience. First, he never gave up and he never compromised his needs. He believed he could find a natural solution to his stress and kept trying.

If something didn't work, he moved on without judging himself as a failure. He never blamed natural medicine for failing to work. He held true to his intuition that something would work.

When something worked a little, he was grateful and looked for something more. All too often, people believe that it is their lot in life to suffer. Yong's can-do attitude made him succeed even before he arrived at the final solution.

Moreover, he changed his lifestyle to reduce stress and became a better student. Mornings were better for clear-headed study. So he switched his study time to make it easier on himself. When stress management tools seemed counter-intuitive to him (ie, walking away from your studies when you are too stressed out), he tried it anyway.

He asked, "What's the worst that will happen if I don't succeed in this one assignment?" This brilliant question allowed him to see things in perspective: the world won't come to an end and for him, it didn't.

See time management + brain entrainment tips on my website, Pinterest, Twitter + Facebook — see page 128

Great virtue can carry all things in the world - social commitment + ethical standards

More from The Hip Guru's™ Guide

Other Books by Swamiji — (available as books and ebooks)

The Ayurveda Encyclopedia: Natural Secrets to Healing, Prevention + Longevity. (Amazon #1 Bestseller — remained on the top 10 list for years)

Bhagavad Gita for Modern Times: Secrets to Attaining Inner Peace and Harmony

Amazon.com Author's Page
http://www.amazon.com/Swami-Sadashiva-Tirtha/e/B00301RK22/ref=ntt_athr_dp_pel_pop_1

Web + Social Media

Website: http://TheHipGurusGuide.com

Book Extras

http://TheHipGurusGuide.com/college-book/ Password: stressfreestudent

My Social Media Links

Facebook
https://www.facebook.com/pages/The-Hip-Gurus-Guide/266046820219821

Twitter
https://twitter.com/TheHipGurusGuid

Pinterest
http://www.pinterest.com/thehipgurusg uid/

LinkedIn
http://www.linkedin.com/in/swamisadas hivatirtha

Youtube
http://www.youtube.com/channel/UC_ QGUsg2Mmr5Dsdsg7l7_DA

About The Hip Guru's™ Guide — Swamiji

Swamiji is a monk who visited India yearly and has studied and taught meditation and yoga for the past 40 years. He has mastered stress management in the personal and corporate arenas.

As a keynote speaker, facilitator, and trainer, he has spoken at the White House Commission on Complementary and Alternative Medicine Policy, Johnson + Johnson in New York, and at various universities and colleges, including Johns Hopkins University, St. George's University School of Medicine, and Penn State.

He is the founder of the Life Success System — a time-tested roadmap — that took four decades to develop. This system changes the stress quotient in minutes and gives the individual an instant way to release stress, clarify visions, and be on top of their game as leaders. It helps people relieve stress, resulting in increased profits for employers and other employees.

Swamiji, The Hip Guru, is available for
College Career Day,
Orientation Day,
Organizational Day,
Leadership Day, Seminars, Keynotes,
Workshops, and Assemblies

Made in the USA
Middletown, DE
03 September 2015